THE DRUM

VOICE OF THE VILLAGE

ONYE ONYEMAECHI

POINTER OAK

Pointer Oak / Tri S Foundation

Distributed by Millichap Books

millichapbooks.com

shamanzone.com

Contributing photographers: Robert Marcus, Karin Helbling. Special thanks for the use of Igboland village photos by Michael Widjaja.

First edition. First printing

Printed in Canada

ISBN 978-1-937462-07-9

This book is dedicated to my beloved mother, Regina Adaugo Onyemaechi, and my late father, Emmanuel Lumanze Onyemaechi, and Brother, Onyewuchi (Chi chi). Their wisdom and example have given me health, strength, and spiritual insight.

I also dedicate this book to my dearest daughter, Sophia, my son, Nnandi, and my sister, Adaku Ikechi. They are the light and love of my life!

ERI GBOLA (EERY BOLAY)

ONE OF THE TRADITIONAL IGBO GREETINGS.

How is your dancing?

ACUPE —
FAN FOR
DANCE

CONTENTS

LISTEN TO AUDIO EXAMPLES OF DRUMMING ONLINE —
BOOKMARK: SHAMANZONE.COM/ONYE

ONYE AND FRANCIS RICO

FOREWORD

Onye Onyemaechi very often dresses in traditional Nigerian Agbada style — impossibly bright, festive Dashikis with small brightly colored round hats — and, he is a striking and dramatic presence!

When he hits the drums, explosive bursts of energy radiate in all directions, shocking flocks of birds into flight, driving the alligators back into the river, and bringing people from miles around to dance to the joyful grooving village rhythms.

He can also be very gentle, just *touching* the drum, eliciting a soft cooing sound that speaks sweetly to the birds nesting in the trees and to the sleeping babies held in their mother's arms.

Onye is an advisor and healer, a man of God, a world musician and performer — and the lightning strikes of his drums and the thunder claps of the prayers he invokes ignite *illumination* deep within the cells of our body, vibrating and energizing us down to our DNA! Onye is a musician of the original explosive brilliant vibration of Creation itself.

Onye once told me at a Ceremony for World Peace held with indigenous elder Joseph Rael on the California North Coast cliffs above the Pacific Ocean:

> It is a misperception that drumming puts you into a trance, or that the purpose of drumming is to induce a trance!
>
> The truth is quite a different story — drumming is a heartbeat of flowing energy, and when your heart is beating and your energy is flowing, you are healthy and capable of taking action in support of your family, your friends, and your own life.

"*Drumming*" Onye said, with a sharp POW of the drum, "*awakens one from the trance.*"

The sound of drums, the rippling flow of rhythms and repeating patterns — awakens our cellular visceral knowledge of Oneness, of connection and dancing synchronicity with all of Creation. We hear and feel the beat *within* us, *surrounding* us — and we experience the truth that the *outside* and the *inside* are the same.

Onye explains, *"This is why, when the deep groove is played, the stars and galaxies can be seen in people's eyes, the trees dance, and the light of God's love reaches to where — healing is called for."*

In the village communities of Nigeria, the certain knowledge of belonging within the community, of belonging to the land, and to the sky — the inner sense of belonging to the cosmos — provides a foundation in Source that our hyper-mobile modern Western so-called civilization simply does not offer us.

It is part of our core misunderstanding about indigenous cultures that we think that they are *quaint* and *colorful*. And we assume that their dances, music, art, and ceremonies expressing vibrant communion with the Divine all evolved because they weren't able to get TV reception out at the remote edges of the world.

We're the one's who need better reception!

Onye describes his personal evolution, *"Even as a child, as a very young child, I was drawn to the drum and took part in all of the welcoming ceremonies — with nonstop drumming for the village newborns — drumming that would go on for days and days outside of the pregnant mother's house in the village.*

"New life was welcomed into the center of the village, into our hearts, into the center of the community and held in the embrace of the drumming. The new mother would be brought into the circle to be celebrated, and the baby would be passed from person to person, each saying, 'Welcome! You are wanted here — we are so happy you have come."

Contrast this with the Western medical model, where children are born to anesthetized women under the supervision of gowned and masked men and the baby is immediately placed in sanitary isolation.

In Nigeria, the common greeting between people is not a cursory, "Hey, how're you doing?" but rather, "My friend, are you dancing in your life? Are you full of music? Are you flowing? How is your health? And your family?" There is no rush to move on and get to the next thing, because instead of life being a series of disconnected *events*, life is *flowing*.

Onye teaches drumming — drumming for healing, for transformation, for transcendence — and his method is to teach drumming as *love in action*.

He is a highly educated man, but because his *intelligence* was shaped by *drumming* rather than by *words*, he is not run, or overrun, by his mind.

When he needs to think, he thinks. Otherwise, his mind is set aside and is quiet, like a special drum that is played only when he wants to figure out airline flight schedules or read a good book!

It is Onye's heart, lovingly connected to the center of Being, that illuminates the path of his life.

With the divine presence invited to join in to every beat of Onye's drumming, obstructions are loosened, and energy begins to move — and as any healer (and any dancer) can tell you, when we *move* we're healthy.

Ancient tribal cultures understood that many problems are unsolvable. Things become broken, and are unfixable, but whatever the situation is, no matter how badly things have turned out, the problem can be accepted and transcended, and the experience can be included and shared in the life of the village.

This wisdom of the village has become necessary and essential to us now, as our world becomes a single community — a global village. The old archetypes of "noble warrior" and "leader" that evolved to govern our isolated, protected, and defended "tribal" structures have become obsolete.

Our world of separate countries and peoples competing for supposedly "limited" resources no longer exists. We are irrevocably connected together in one world. We are all here *with* each other, sharing every aspect of our relationships with all of life.

"Yes!" Onye says, *"Each beat of the drum says, Yes! Each heartbeat says, Yes! Each breath says, Yes! Creation opens and says, Yes, and so do you, when you say, Yes!"*

Notice that Onye does not say that you must be accurate, perfect, or even competent. He does not say that you must *work* to master drumming — he only suggests that you begin fresh in every moment by saying, *"Yes!"*

As you read and begin to practice the wisdom traditions that Onye offers you here as his gift to our emerging new world, keep the simplicity of this, *"Yes!"* close to your heart, and let it guide you to the profound joy of your own free flowing *Celebration* of life!

FRANCIS RICO

C WELCOME

ome. Come with me to my village.

I have lived in the West for many years, but I still feel the pulse of the village drum. When I drum, I can leave my body and go back — back to the village. We are connected in that pulse, and I feel everyday what is happening those many thousands of miles away. My village in Nigeria and my home in California are woven together. I can feel the pulse and hear each heart beat.

The tribe I was born into in Africa is Igbo and in our village we practice the old ways. We share everything with the drum.

In my village every child is welcomed into the world with the drum. When my mother went into labor with me, someone in the village started to beat the birth song on the village drum. The song says, "The one we have been waiting for is here. Come and welcome the one we have been waiting for."

1

FERTILITY
MASK

When the woman is pregnant, or maybe even before conception, the village or the elder persons or even someone in the extended family circle would have an inclination, a sort of premonition of who is coming to be born even before the pregnancy. It's amazing how it works. The people, especially of the Igbo tribe, don't talk a lot about the mysteries. You live the mysteries. The mysteries become a part of the existence and the tradition. And that's how it is passed down from one generation to the next.

The woman got pregnant. She goes through the whole process, nine months. And there's a lot that goes on during that time. She continues her way of living. She does her work on the farm and she's honored and respected by anyone she comes in contact with. People in the village will go out of their way to assist the woman with whatever she may need. As the time is getting closer, the woman will continue to do her chores and go to the market or take care of the family. As the time for the child comes closer and the women have the intuition that it is time for the spirit of the child to come out into the world. Relations and relatives that live very far away suddenly travel to the village with food or wood or whatever gifts they may have. People start arriving unannounced. When they arrive — maybe two or three or four days later — the child is already coming, and you hear a sound that the woman's about to have a child. All the women will come together immediately and the announcement will go faster than the postal services. The drums will go off — people playing the drums announcing to the villagers that a child is coming to Earth. And the children and the young girls and the women will gather around her while she's having this child. The village will spontaneously play music and songs while she's going through the labor until the child arrives. When the child is arriving out of the womb, the sound of the drum allows the child to cry or to show a sign of life. Usually in the West, you spank the child to force the breathing, but the sound

of the drum will wake the child up to give its first cry that he or she has arrived!

The child is then washed by the midwife and carried to the mother. After the mother has connected with the child, the father will throw the child in the air and catch the child. Then the child is turned upside down and gently shaken. This helps the child remove birth trauma and signifies that the child is strong, healthy, and has arrived to his native land.

When this newborn cries it signifies that he is alive and is in his body. This child is awakened in his body and this is very important because this child is already learning to trust the wisdom of his physical being. Every cell in the body of this child is being called by the drum to wake up to the potential of physical life on this planet. I want you to understand this because this potential in the human

ONYE AS A
BABY WITH
HIS MOTHER

ONYE AS A
BABY WITH
HIS MOTHER

3

LISTEN

body is being carried forward by this child as a gift to himself, to his tribe, and, I believe, as a gift from this tribe to all humankind. As I tell you my story you will come to understand how this is true.

The cry of the child is a joyful cry to the family, the village, the community, and the world. The birth of a child is considered a sacred and solemn rite. Everyone in the village is praying for a successful and healthy delivery. Some first cries are gentle, quiet, and soft; some are intense. I believe the first cry indicates the power and intensity of the child's energetic nature. The mother or the father of the infant will announce the birth by singing to everyone like this . . . Haaaaay, haaaaay, hay, hay, hay, haaaay hay.

The music and the singing continues to go on. Then the family of the father will give a white powder called NZU to everyone to lick and make a mark on their neck and face to signify the new child has arrived. Nzu means "white chalk" and signifies purity of heart, goodwill, holiness and welcome.

Someone in the gathering will ask, "Is it a boy, girl, twin, triplets?" The women who helped with the birth will confirm the gender and everyone gathered will acknowledge and congratulate the woman and child and give praise to the Almighty God for a healthy new child. You have all these people — one hundred people, two hundred people, three hundred people, music, dance, and food.

Now, when the child has arrived, an elder person, it could be a man or a woman, will lift the child up to the sky, presenting this child to God. They will call the spirit of the ancestors of the village. They will in the spirit of the child's ancestors by calling out the names of the ones who have died. This is the tradition.

This is the lineage this child comes from. The mother will give a temporary name to the child. The name will change at some point in the child's life depending on how he or she behaves. That name becomes a personal name, and says something about the character, the values, the principles the child holds the rest of his life or her life.

After the celebration the mother and the child will be on a healing retreat for three months to renew her body and soul. During this time the woman is nourished with traditional foods and herbal medicines to heal and regain her strength. The child will be breast fed until it is able to make the transition to solid food. This is a very significant time when mother and child bond peacefully with each other.

When I say the drum wakes the infant up, you can start to understand how I use drumming now. The drum will awaken your body, heart and soul. The drum will bring you to the present in this life. That's because the echoes of the drum invites all possibilities. It corrects and rebalances all situations. When you are sad or even

ONYE'S FATHER AND MOTHER

when you are happy, it just clears things, brings you to a point of entry and departure where you can be reunited within your soul.

Every cell in your body can be awakened to the Sacred Center of the cosmos. You, like me, have a drum inside you that connects you to the original sound vibration of creation. The drum that is inside of you can birth you into this holy world of connection.

SINCE I GREW UP IN THE VILLAGE, I share the village perspective on how birth should be celebrated. I revere the mother and child connection as a sacred union of body, soul, heart, mind, and spirit. It is my wish for all women giving birth and all children being born to be welcomed and honored. My wish is for the women, young girls, fathers and young boys, elderly women and elderly men, to gather around the woman having the child. Together you sing and play sacred music with strings, flutes and drum, and dance to the beat of the birthing contractions. The heart intelligence of each of you is then awakened and enlivened with excitement and jubilation in this ecstatic celebration of life.

A mother's power, using all her internal might and strength to deliver her child into the world, is a miraculous act. This miracle of life is an internal music similar to the precious moment of the creation of the cosmos. In the beginning was the Word and then the word was made flesh — embodied sound. All emerged from the Only One Source, issuing forth first as sound.

The echo of the drum penetrates the psyche and operates in profound ways familiar and mysterious. Drumming is a spiritual practice that represents the heartbeat and the soul.

I was my Father's first child — the eldest son. He was proud and happy to have such a healthy, vibrant, active, and curious child. I awakened in him a sense of great responsibility for ensuring that I learned the lessons of life so that I would be prepared to face the challenges that he knew were ahead.

I had the love, support, and encouragement of my Grandfather, who was a deep spiritual presence in our extended family and village, and of my Great Uncle Dey, who taught me the ways of nature, beginning when I was first able to walk and explore the world.

BABY ONYE

I will teach you about the forms and ancient traditions of the tribal village. They are still to be valued, respected and cherished, but this book is not about the past. It is my intention in this book to call in the new song, the drumming heartbeat of life itself that has the power and the energy to restore connection, wholeness, wellbeing, sanity, love, kindness, and cooperation to our global civilization, our global village.

Part One

BECOME PRESENT WITH THE DRUM

I saw wings start to spread and come in from the other side while I was drumming just now. At first I thought it must be an eagle, then I realized it has a face so it can't be an eagle. It must be an angel — an angel has come through the drum to meet us. That's the prayer.

So the prayer has come into this room as an angel — the prayer invited the angel from the world of Spirit to come to meet us. This really affirms what we are doing — life itself is asking us to become present with the drum.

So, thank you. I thank you, starting with your family, because you were born in this time and place to be a part of this circle right now.

I was the first son from two big families in my African village. I was the first grandchild born to both of these families, so my birth was very significant to this community.

They all came together to bless my arrival.

5
LISTEN

There was certainly drumming on the day I was born, but my experience of drumming goes back even further than being born. I have very old memories about being in my mother's womb.

EVERYWHERE SHE WENT, THERE I WAS, participating already in all aspects of her life and the life of the village. When I was a boy she would often say to me, "You were always kicking around in my stomach, especially when people were talking and playing music. I think you were already playing the drum." She had a sense that this child in her womb was already a social person — a child that enjoys music and understands the rhythm of the drum.

I have always had a special relationship to my mother. She could pretty much sense when I was not happy, when I was upset, or when I was feeling happy. She would just know — she's highly intuitive.

GRANDMOTHER, MOTHER AND ONYE

My grandparents were also very influential in my life. It was interesting. My father's mother was a different kind of a person — she was more serious than my mother, more intense, stern, and businesslike. She was always thinking ahead about the future — what is to come. She would ask me the sticky, sometimes uncomfortable questions. Where are you now? Where do you want to be in five years? Do you have any plans? I understand why my father has that ability to look into the future and to set goals and to plan. My father's mother has to plan everything. She always has a plan.

My father got that from her. He was a very powerful individual, very intelligent. He was an engineer, architect, and businessman.

The grandmother who was involved in the spiritual side of my childhood was my mother's mother, my maternal grandmother. She was a very calm and very wise woman. People came to her to get her advice and to be comforted.

PEOPLE COME TO MY FATHER'S MOTHER, too, but for a different kind of help. She can be intimidating at times, because she is very clear about what she expects. Unscrupulous individuals are afraid to come to her because she can read their character and intentions and says to them, "Get out of here! We have nothing in common. I have nothing to say to you."

My mother is the one with the healing ability. That's where I got it—from my mother. She has that power. I think her mother might have had that gift as well, but my grandmother chose to be the wise woman in the village instead of the healer. She is now an elder, very wise and very caring, kind and compassionate.

ONYE'S FATHER AND PATERNAL GRANDMOTHER   ONYE'S GRANDFATHER

DRUMMING IS MY OWN SPECIAL GIFT. I was drumming in my mother's womb. When you are a child in your mother's womb, you hear all sorts of things. You hear everything. My mother knew about me, about who I was and who I have become. I think I knew about her in some special ways, too. She told me that I had been an uncle to her in a past life. Something happened and I died, but before I died I promised that when I was born in my next life, I would come back to my mother. So it was I, my mother's uncle that had passed away while my mother was still alive, that now came back to her as a child.

ONYE'S FATHER

And this is the way the fabric of my community continues itself and recognizes and remembers each other. People in the village say they recognized me when I was born, so certainly my mother knew who I was.

It makes a lot of sense that to this day my relationship with my mother is very solid without the need to be in the same place and to communicate physically. All we have to do is just feel the deep connection. I talked to her on the telephone yesterday. She said, "My son, I haven't heard from you physically. You haven't called me physically." I said, "I understand, Mama, but you've heard me." She said, "Yes." So we don't speak a lot. A lot of the communication is done in the spiritual world. Then we speak very briefly and she blesses me, and she prays for me, and she hangs up the phone. We don't talk a lot. Most of the communication is done already in the spirit.

She has given her blessing to this work.

I NEVER LEARNED HOW TO PLAY THE DRUM. Nobody ever taught me how to drum here on this plane. It's more something that I am, that was acquired or inherited in the spiritual realms. That is still how I receive teachings and information. That's how I learned about sound, frequencies, and vibrations. So, when I play, the teachings are being translated into notes. The information is revealed. Whatever sound that comes represents the language of spirit in the moment it is translated. So, it is very important to be in tune with spirit when you translate the rhythm. You have to be in tune to pure vibration.

Of course, everybody drums in the village and I naturally enjoyed that sound vibration. All I needed was a drum and I started playing.

And the drum sounds just started coming out of me.

When I was around five, six, or seven years old, my friend and I would go to play hide-and-seek at a school that was near the village. My friends and I would just go out there for hours to play all kinds of games. We would often stay until sunset. Once everybody left but me and I was left behind, alone. A man suddenly showed up. He was dressed in white; he was a black man, of course, but he was wearing only white. He looked very distinguished, and was a nice looking man. He said to me, "Son, do you mind giving me a ride on your bicycle to this location?" I knew the location he was speaking of. There was a house there. I knew that nobody lived in that house, and I had often wondered who had ever lived there. My friends and I often said to each other that ghosts lived in the house. None of us had ever visited that house. It wasn't far, so I said he could ride on my bicycle with me and I would take him there.

ONYE WITH
A FRIEND IN
AFRICA

We never got to that house. He told me to let him off when we were about ten meters away. I started to pedal away but then turned around to watch him enter the house, but the man had disappeared. I thought, "how can this man disappear that quickly?" I suspected that this man was a spirit or an angel — someone from another dimension. I started peddling away from that place and I peddled so quickly that I soon landed back in my family's compound in the village, and I crashed and dropped on the ground. My grandmother came up to me and said, "Where have you been? What's going on? What have you done?" I told her what happened.

She asked me, "Were you respectful?"

I said, "Yes."

"Were you kind to the man?"

I said, "Yes."

"Did he give you a blessing?"

I remembered that the man did bless me when I dropped him off. He said, "Thank you for giving me a ride. May God bless you the rest of your life."

My grandmother said, "That is good. He was a spirit, a guest from the other side. You will be blessed and lucky all of your life."

I have never forgotten that visitation, and it made me feel the presence of the world of spirit all around me.

IN THE VILLAGE THE YOUNG MEN ARE SEPARATED into a group their own age. The age groups remain together the rest of their lives. They do things together and support each other during hard times. They talk about the important issues going on in their lives and the initiation they face before becoming a man. They stay together and they are always there for one another. They make music together, dance, cook, play, and spend time together in the forest. We spent a lot more time in the forest than at home. We spent much more time in the forest than a modern child spends on a playground. Our playground was the forest where we were always

in harmony with the plants, the animals, and especially the trees.

I believe wild animals are, in a way, wiser than human beings. They are in tune with the earth and understand how to listen to the earth to know how to survive. They know what to eat and where to go in different seasons. They know how to move and they know if there is going to be a big event like an earthquake or a tidal wave. They are very respectful of boundaries and sometimes they collaborate and cooperate with each other.

My Great Uncle Dey was a quiet man, but there was something about him that brought people to him — he was loved and respected by everyone who knew him. He was the most skilled sculptor and carver and prolific master of drum making in the village. He was a true artist. His depth of knowledge regarding nature — particularly his knowledge and love for trees — was extensive and comprehensive. He taught me to pray for the trees, and he would speak to his ancestors and pray before cutting a tree down to make a drum, or furniture or beautiful art for our homes.

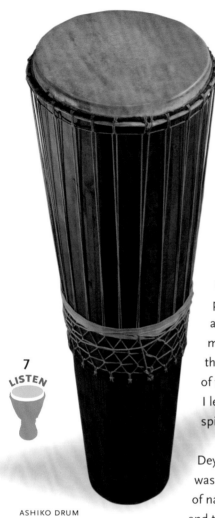

7

LISTEN

ASHIKO DRUM

Great Uncle Dey shared his deep reverence for nature with me, his sense of loving connectedness and understanding of the ways of every form of being — from trees to the rocks, ponds, vines, insects, birds and creatures of every kind — all of life was sacred to Great Uncle Dey.

I was a curious child, I would spend many hours just absorbing Dey's wisdom. He could predict if a tree is diseased or healthy by touching, tasting the bark, and smelling it. If a tree was not well, he would pray for it to regain life force and to grow abundantly. Dey taught me to sense the magnetic field of the sound associated with the drum tree. Also, I can tell from the sound of the drum the origin of the tree it came from. I learned that every tree tells its story through spirit and the powerful sound of the drum. What I learned, just by being with Uncle Dey, became very helpful when as a child I was allowed to directly experience the wisdom of nature, to be alone with all of the plants and trees and creatures that live in the tropical forest. This was an initiation into discovery of our true relationship with Creation that was normally reserved for young men.

That morning I was awakened early from my sleep and told to dress and follow my elder into the forest. My friends and I often played in the forest so I was happy to be there until I realized he had left and now I was alone. I became alert to every being, whether tree, plant, bird, reptile, or animal. At first I was upset and cried, but as time went by I began to wonder what to do. I was much further into the tropical forest than I had ever been. I was thirsty and sleepy.

I watched the animals to see what they did. I noticed the monkeys went to drink water that pooled between the roots of a large tree. When I was so thirsty my tongue got fat in my throat I kneeled at the foot of that tree and scooped up water with my hands.

I watched to see where the monkeys would sleep. I saw several monkeys high up in the tree so I climbed up until I found a comfortable wide limb. A lot of time passed, so that I no longer cried, thought about time, or wondered when someone would come to find me.

When I was hungry I watched the animals, especially the monkeys, to see what they would eat, and I ate what they ate. I slept, held in the arms of the trees. I played with twigs and branches. I splashed water on my face. I prayed for the wellbeing of all the animals and plants I met, and, in time with the rhythm of the tropical forest, I drummed.

The experience blessed me with inner strength, power, wisdom, patience, and endurance as well as the certain knowledge that I was one with life.

Meanwhile, back in our Village, my Father, Mother, Grandparents, Great Uncle Dey, and everyone else in the village danced and prayed for me, to keep me safe. Everyone expected me to return on my own when my initiation in the tropical forest was over.

Eventually I found my way back to the village, and there was a big celebration! As this experience blessed me, a child of the Village, it blessed the Village too. Through the strength of its growing children, life is renewed within the family and within the village.

EACH COMPOUND IN THE VILLAGE HAS A SQUARE HUT, called an Obi.

The houses in the Village are small, so to accommodate several people you need a meeting house. The best place to put the Obi, or the meeting house, is in the middle of the compound. This is where we go to address issues that pertain to the family and the elders come to pass wisdom to the younger ones. Here is where we tell stories of the ancestors. This is the place family members come for meetings or where the elders of the village come to resolve legal, social, and economic issues for the community. Before any case can commence both the plaintiff and the defendant must swear in front of everyone present an oath to the ancestral spirits to tell only the truth.

ONYE'S MASK

And it's also a place where the forefathers who have passed on come at night to watch over their children and their families. It is also a place to come to talk about issues that matter to us, a place to heal. My grandfather on my father's side always comes to this hut at night when everybody else is asleep. As a child I watched for him to go to the hut, then I would go and sit with him in the middle of the night. One night I went to sit with my grandfather and there was a man with him. I could hear them talking. I slipped in to sit with him and find out whom he was talking to. Then I realized it was nobody in this dimension. He was just talking to the spirits. So I sat with him all night. And sometimes he would notice I was there and sometimes he would not, because he was already in the spirit world talking to his ancestors. In the village, we understood that we are multi-dimensional beings living a human experience on this plane. We understood that we could travel on the spiritual plane and on the emotional plane and on the energetic plane to parallel realities.

It was natural for me to develop the ability to communicate with

8
LISTEN

the spiritual realm. I was never taught that this was not possible. I was taught that this was normal and good—a blessing.

When my grandfather went to the Obi he was just conversing with his ancestors. It wasn't what you would think of as a prayer. It was like a prayer, but also like a conversation. He could ask, "Bless my family" or "Bless my community." There was a dialogue going on. You could call it a prayer.

I think of it as sacred talk that involves family and community, and it also involves normal, daily things that happen. It is interacting personally with the spirit of those who have gone before. This was where I came to understand the spiritual world. While my grandfather was having this conversation, I was part of it spiritually as well. I'm in it, but separate from the way my grandfather is in it, because he has traveled to a different dimension in his spiritual communication. I could witness his travel but I was too young to go fully with him. I could hear the voices but I couldn't always understand. It was enough for me to be near him and to wait for him to translate what the spirits had told him. Sometimes he would gather the family and tell them, and sometimes he would not. When Grandfather wanted to tell the elders a story from his visit to the other side they would gather in the Obi.

I would try to get in, but they would kick me out. I would think, "What is it they are hiding from me? What is this secret? What are they talking about? What is this wisdom? What do they have?" I was curious, and because of my experience with my grandfather I wanted to be there and to know. The elders would kick me out and I would sneak back in.

Finally one of the elders said, "Just leave him alone. Let him come in so that way we don't get distracted from our meeting."

So they let me into their meeting. When they started this meeting they would call out the kola nut. It's a very significant gesture in the Igbo family tradition. The kola nut symbolizes peace. It comes from a kola nut tree. This nut has ridges that naturally divide into three, four, or five pieces. The youngest person in the group is given the kola nut to split it and share it with the others according

KOLA NUT
CEREMONY

to age. The eldest man would bless the nut before everybody partook in communion with it. It represents community, peace, and ceremony. This is a very important ritual in the Igbo tradition. When they let me into the meeting, I got to be a part of that ceremony. As I was the youngest, I got to divide the nut to share it with the others. That signified acceptance of me as a member of the group, and from me it signified a respect for the elders.

In Western civilization the old and the sick are often removed from the home and from the community. In our tribe the elders are taken care of and given respect and honor, even after they have passed from this world into the next.

KOLA NUT CEREMONY

Attending a kola nut ceremony is one of the most important of gatherings of the Igbo people. The kola nut tradition is used for a wide range of events, but principally to welcome guests to a village, into a home, or to a meeting. However, the ceremony may vary depending on the occasion and the community present at the ceremony.

The kola nut symbolizes peace, fellowship, and brotherhood. In every gathering, a kola nut must be presented first before any program can commence. Usually, it is respectful that the eldest person bless the kola nuts.

He takes the kola nuts with his right hand and offers blessings, prayers or a toast by using a native proverb: "A good fortune follows a good person."

Then, the youngest person in the gathering breaks the kola with his hands or with a knife. The breaking of the kola nuts is one of the most significant aspects of the entire ceremony. When the kola nut is broken, the number of parts it splits into has great meaning.

If the kola nuts fall into two parts, it signals that the hostess has suspicious motives — or it's just bad luck or a bad omen! A kola nut that breaks into four parts is considered good, and usually denotes the four market days of Igboland. Five or more parts means prosperity and fortune for the host family.

At this time, the purpose of the gathering is announced, while the kola nuts are being distributed to everyone. Sometimes, native palm wine, garden eggs, and peanut butter are presented as well. One can dip the kola nut into the peanut butter and eat it!

This Igbo tradition continues the full respect for the elders that is part of every important gathering and is shared in the villages. This tradition of respect is the reason we have strong connections to the ancestors.

Kola nuts hold sacred significance in the Igbo social life.

The kola nut diminishes hunger and fatigue, energizes you, and also keeps you awake with it's natural caffeine.

The Igbo believe that the kola nut symbolizes pure intention, peace, brotherhood, and connects us to our ancestors.

The breaking kola nuts ceremony is almost unavoidable for anyone visiting any Igbo person.

A kola nut breaking marks the beginning of any important occasion for the Igbos.

Breaking kola nut is a tradition that creates a bond of shared ceremony.

Elders agree that once kola nuts are blessed with prayers, the visitors will know that they are welcome.

If there are no kola nuts, the host/ hostess is obligated to apologize and offer an alternative.

The kola nut is used to settle disputes between siblings, neighbors or friends.

Any Kola nut which has two segments is not served in Igboland. It signifies bad luck or a bad omen.

Like the saying goes, "Onye wetara Oji, wetara Ndu," which means, "He who brings kola nut, certainly brings life to the present moment."

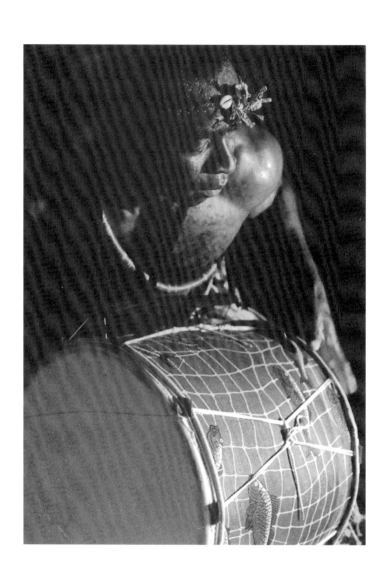

Part Two

HEALING WITH
THE DRUM

I didn't start to use the drum as
a form of healing when I was young.
It happened later on. I did use the
knowledge and the wisdom of sound and its
capacity to draw in healing and transformation
from the things I learned in the village I grew up in. As a boy I

NIGERIAN CLAY
DRUM

enjoyed music and certain ceremonial events, not just for my
entertainment, but for my own internal development. I knew even
then that when I played, something shifted in the energy around
the sound, and people realized there was a change. I never made
a big deal out of it until later in my life. As I was maturing in my
spiritual understanding, I was being introduced into the spiritual
realms where I could hear sounds playing or hear groups of people
playing the drum. So, I was being shown all of this in the spiritual
dimension. That is where a lot of my training comes from.

In the later part of my life when I realized the power and the
energy that constitutes the sound of the drum and saw the effect
it has on people, then I started allowing myself to be present for
it. The drum kept revealing itself, and I kept discovering its power
and potential to help people come into themselves in a stronger,
healthier way.

Through drumming I started to be able to move from the normal
world into the dimension of spirit. That's when rhythms and
patterns would start to emerge, and the vibration would bring the
call of the sacred.

I came to this country to study, not to do healing. My Father sent
me to college because he wanted me to have a serious career. He

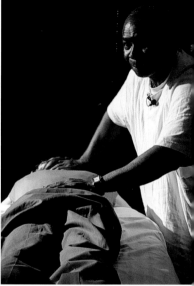

wanted me to be reading books and studying to be an architect or an engineer and he considered drumming and healing a distraction.

9
LISTEN

WHEN I WAS IN COLLEGE, I ran track, and I had friends who were athletes. Sometimes one of them would get injured or break a bone, then I place my hands above their injury. I could feel their injury in my hands. If they had a sprained ankle, it would come into my hands tingling like a vibrating frequency of sound and their ankle or other injury would improve. The athletes would say, "So, you are a voodoo doctor?" and I would say, "No, no. I'm not a voodoo doctor. This is just God's work through me happening to you." And for sure, they would be healed.

That gave me a deeper insight into the healing possibilities of drumming or any kind of music that could transfer that frequency of energy from one person to another. If this frequency of energy could be transmitted to another person, it could cancel out any difficulties and dispel negative energy so that their own body could adjust and heal.

That was the beginning and I see it happening now more and more in all kinds of situations and circumstances, with people of all races and belief systems.

Once I was in North Carolina at a workshop and conference. Rabbis and ministers and different religious denominations were there, drumming together, when the voice of the drum led me to one particular individual.

Through the sound, I could tell this person, a woman, had problems with her spine. I could tell that at some point in her life her spinal cord had been injured and she was having problems at this particular time. I started drumming and coming closer to her. She kept moving away from me. I just kept following her because I kept feeling the vibration of the sound adjusting her spine. I could not explain how this was happening, but I could feel the shifts in the sound as it is transmitted into this person's body doing what it needed to do. At that particular time, it happened to be her spine. The drum adjusted her spine and straightened her spine out. Later on when we finished the drumming and dancing she testified that she felt the drum vibrating in her body and adjusting her spine. Everyone was amazed. I wasn't amazed, because I could feel what the drum was doing and I knew what was happening. I have been with the drum with a person who was in a coma and witnessed the sound of the drum drawing the person out of the coma state back to awareness and life.

I BELIEVE EVERYBODY HAS THE POWER TO HEAL. I believe everyone can come into a healing relationship with the drum. It's a gift. God blessed us all with an enormous amount of power to heal, to see, and to prophesize. It's just a matter of following this calling. If you are called to do this work, it is much easier to be trained in it. If you are called to this work it is easier to perceive the intricate and complex vibration of the spiritual world and to facilitate interaction between the spiritual and the physical world.

Healing is available to everyone. It is a God-given gift, but you must awaken to it and develop it.

I LOVE ANYTHING THAT HAS TO DO WITH THE MYSTERY OF GOD. I'm curious to know how the energy from different dimensions intertwines and functions. How can we use these energies to do good? If we all are gifted by God to do good, why not develop that gift? If we use that gift regularly, the world will be a different and better place, with less war and more community.

Drumming is multidimensional and I want to show you how to use different vibrations of the drum to awaken different dimensions in the body. A very important dimension awakened by drumming is the original, authentic self.

When a person drums, something special awakens in him that is unique to that individual. What awakens is the core aspect of the individual's existence. That awakenness is what I see as a constant flame. It is a reminder to each of us that we are alive. We are in co-existence with divinity. We are sacred. We are whole. When the flame core path awakens, we are energized, we are in divine health, we are able to do miracles and to experience the sacredness of our own lives.

What you used to think of as miraculous becomes your normal state because you are in tune with the divine Creator. The Bible in Genesis tells about the many beginnings; the beginning of the universe, the beginning of man and woman and the beginning of family relationships; the beginning of relationships to our ancestors, and most of all, the beginning of the breath of life. Since the dawn of creation, we have been part of this unfolding mystery. The awakening of our self and all creation through sound allows us to come into form and then to be pushed toward a clear perception of our oneness with the Divine.

Drumming is a sacred language. By drumming we grow our own roots into sacred connection with Source. In Western culture we feel separated from our heart, which is our own personal drum, and out of separation we feel separated from each other. Drumming grows roots from our heart into the sacred heart of the divine. If you were to pull a tree out of the ground, you would see the roots. Some are delicate. Some are strong. They come in various dimensions — different and separate ways, individually but very strong.

When you drum, you grow roots into the divine. Some are delicate. Some are strong. Some are powerful. While you are drumming these roots reach from your energetic heart into the energetic heart of the divine community. The sounds create a vibrant, powerful community that includes everyone in the world from all races and cultures. Imagine the biggest tree as the universe and we are all under its roots participating individually with these roots and drumming to its strength and power in the world.

When you drum in community, you are bringing yourself to the group and the group to yourself.

Drumming to celebrate life and just to enjoy is part of the mystery. That's what celebration is about. Festivity, joy, sacredness — all are part of divinity. We are meant to have fun in life and to enjoy each other.

I WANT TO TALK ABOUT DRUMMING AS A TOOL to awaken from the trance of modern civilization, the trance of technology, and the trance of media. We are in a modern civilization that has created so much distraction with technology and with media that people have lost touch with the world inside themselves. Drumming is a way to come out of that trance.

In our world of connection through technology, everyone is focused on their little gadgets. We are losing touch with our body wisdom and heart fire. The drum brings us back home to ourselves and wakes up our cellular memory.

Many people think that drumming puts you into a trance, but the drum does not put you into a trance. It awakens you out of the trance state. It is pure and clear, loud and clear. When you awaken, you are consciously aware of your participation in your own life and in the lives of others. There is no confusion about it. When you are in a trance state, you lose focus. When you are in trance you are not yourself and you cannot think for yourself. Being in a cultural trance, living in the world of technology, creates a lot of problems, because you are not in control of your body, your mind, your heart, or your destiny. But if you awaken and are conscious, you can make discerning judgments and decisions that affect all of your life.

DRUMMING IS A PATH TO WHOLENESS, healing, and awakening. I am describing coming back — coming back into your senses, your precious body. This is the gift that is available when you do this work.

To become whole is to become holy. You can love another human being unconditionally, and you feel love for yourself. Your health is strong. Your mind is in the right place. Your actions are right. You stand in right relationship to the divine realms, on a sacred and holy ground, in a state of reverence for all that is. If you are wholesome and holy in this way, your life goal is to be of service to others. When you serve others they feel the wholeness and divinity in you and something shifts in them. It is miraculous.

When this shift happens the ones you have served can come into their own wholeness/holiness and can make their unique contribution to the world. When they stand in that positive shift and touch another human being, then the person touched also comes into right relationship and can come into their own power to do something good, something positive. The ripple effect goes on.

The insanity of our times, the mental illness, is that people are separated from each other, from all aspects of their humanity. They are anesthetized and they are numb and coming out of that state, being touched by the ripple, brings you out of the numbness and back in touch with your life. That's what is healing. Without that no amount of pharmaceutical drugs can bring you to wholeness or to holiness. The holiness is in the sound itself. The sound becomes the element you bring into your being that energizes you and aligns you in a state of good health.

THE SOUND NURTURES YOU SPIRITUALLY. It heals depression of the body's health and brings a powerful surge of energy to your mind and all the organs in your body. All your organs are communicating with each other because your soul and your spirit are in a place of peace, wholeness and holiness.

I believe the insanity of separation in our Western culture starts at birth when a newborn child is separated from the mother in a sterile and impersonal medical environment. That separation happens so early. I believe the way of the village is better, because the child is surrounded by a village who loves and welcomes him. In the village the child is celebrated no matter what condition the child is in coming into the world. This child is celebrated with love. This child is celebrated with the sound of the drum, chanting, music, that connects the aliveness in the root of this child's beating heart to the beating heart of the community.

The child is passed around and welcomed wholeheartedly. We believe in the rebirth of the soul. It is hard to explain the feeling of being born in the body again — the surprise. You are gone for a long time and suddenly you show up. You haven't been seen this many years and suddenly you show up. "Oh, I know you. Welcome back." And with utmost joy the village receives you with the best heart that involves music and drumming and dance. The village really and truly sees you like never before. I believe it would be wonderful everywhere if a woman going into labor were surrounded by prayer, music, songs, and chanting. When the child is about to come into the world, he should hear more music, more drumming, dancing and celebrating as he arrives with his ecstatic cry for life, all of these elements should welcome this child into this world as a gift to God and a blessing for all of us to have.

MIRACLES ARE PART OF OUR EVERYDAY LIFE but we don't perceive them because we haven't learned how to receive the extraordinary or to hear the miraculous. I want to help you see with the eyes of the spirit and hear with the ears of the soul. The

first thing I want to suggest is that you go into nature, a forest or a hilltop, or just your backyard. Stand in the light — just recognize the light. Hear the wind — just hear the breath of the earth. This is sacred. Bring awareness of the sacred into your everyday. Don't wait until you are in crisis to cry out the name of God. See God every day in everything. Include Spirit in all the small things in your life. This is the first way to develop your own gift for perceiving and co-creating miracles.

IF YOU GO BACK TO GENESIS, the Word of God is sound, and that sound is what brings us into form on this earth, on this physical plane. That alone is a miracle. We exist. We are blessed and anointed in this miracle of life. We forget this miracle of being alive in our body and look outside to trust someone or something else to tell us how to be alive. But the miracle is you. The miracle begins with you. When you make the connection with divinity, the miracle is profound and expanded. The manifestation of it is just in our everyday existence. Getting up in the morning is a miracle, and continuing your day is a miracle. Everything you do all day is a miracle and on and on until you return back to God. When you go into sleep, you are returning to Divinity until the next day. How do we conjure such a miracle as our life every day? It is a gift given us by the Divine when we are born.

What we ask for is already manifested. The moment we shout or speak its name it is already happening. Pray as if your prayer is already answered. It is a miracle. And it happens all the time. It is the evocation, the calling of the sound frequencies. It's about sound. All our existence is about sound. Without sound we don't exist. It is this sound in which the universe was created and all manifestation was created. That's why the sound of the drum is sacred, holy and wholesome.

It is the call of the heart beating at the center of all creation.

All around us is sound, and even while we sleep we are consumed with divine sound.

I LOVE WORKING WITH CHILDREN. I love being invited to schools or parks to create a replica of the village where I grew up in Africa. I love taking the children to this place. I have them wear costumes and learn to drum and dance and I make a point of including everybody. We bring everybody in. We make it all one village.

Last week I created an African village for an assembly in a school in Santa Rosa, California. The children were all dressed in African garb and were singing and dancing and drumming. While we were all drumming together as a community, I sensed something had happened not long ago at the school. Maybe there had been a death or something like that. I could feel grieving, and the grieving was so heavy. The grief was manifest in the sound we were creating so I said, "Let's all come together to celebrate loss, whatever we may have lost." Then one of the children spoke up, "We lost a friend, a student last week in a car accident." I knew then that all the students in the school were grieving. Together we understood that was the point of the celebration. We celebrated the grief of the ones in that school through music and words of wisdom. We brought the school family together for healing, not only for themselves but also for the family of the child who had passed. It was a really special gathering. The principal and everyone was very moved. It was a miracle that we had all come together at this moment. It was a miracle in the everyday life.

There are many stories of miracles that have happened to me with school children. Sometimes when I have a program at a school one of the teachers will be pregnant, and I will give a special blessing for her and her child at the end of the assembly. I will have the pregnant teacher (sometimes there may be more than one, even two or three) come to the center of a circle. All the female teachers will surround her, then all the children will circle round, and then all the male teachers and staff. We will drum and chant and sing songs together. I explain to her that this is a blessing for her child, that she have a successful birth, and that this child will be healthy and have a happy and blessed life. Then we close with a gong.

I am always paying attention to spirit, so I can be aware of all of the information that is coming in to energize or to bring some form of transformation to the group whether with children at a school or in the corporate situation. I just pay attention to what instruction is given to me to change the frequency of the energy at that present moment.

When I am in a school and there is a child there with a disability or who is in a wheelchair, I make a special point to include them in the same way as the other children so they do not feel separated. What usually happens is the child will come in a wheelchair and be pushed to the side. I will bring this child in the wheelchair into the circle with everyone. Everyone will be together and we all will be dancing with the one in the wheelchair around with everybody else. Sometimes the teacher will be afraid that somebody is going to get hurt, but tell them not to worry and that everything will be just fine. We are in a peaceful environment where no one is thinking negative thoughts against each other. It is just about love and celebration and music. When we are relaxed and happy it is amazing what happens. Singing and dancing in their African costumes, the students come alive. The one in the wheelchair is not stooped down

any longer and will sing, a sign of joy. And all the kids will come over to the one in the wheelchair and touch him and hold his hands whereas they would never do that before. It's really fascinating what happens. We are all happy when we are all included.

All children need a place where they feel loved and someone cares about them. They need a place where they have the freedom to move their bodies. It is hard to sit still and listen with your ears and not have your whole body included. In my assemblies everyone is a dancer. Everyone is a villager. Everyone becomes a member of the community.

I REMEMBER AN INCIDENT AT ONE OF MY VILLAGE ASSEMBLIES. A teacher had been out of her classroom sick for some time. A substitute teacher had taken over for her. When I came into the classroom, I sensed the interaction between the substitute teacher and the students was off balance. There was no clear communication between them. I could also sense the puzzlement from the substitute teacher. I started using music and drumming and dance to bring the kids and the substitute teacher together as a village. I created a place where they could speak from their heart. In that setting the children were able to speak the truth. The kids were having a hard time and were grieving about their teacher being ill and not being there with them. The substitute teacher didn't know how to help them acknowledge their feelings

and their emotions so there was a problem for the kids until they came into an environment where they felt safe enough, loved enough, and supported enough to speak their truth. After they were able to do this and the teacher was able to acknowledge this, they came together as a village and there was peace.

It is a big problem in our schools when there is no place for the children to speak the truth in their hearts. After the kids were able to say what they were feeling they were able to cry. Even the substitute teacher had tears in her eyes. She had been having a hard time expressing how she really felt to the students. Given a supported space the students were ready to receive her. The student aids had also been having difficulties because they were caught in the confusion and felt as if they were outsiders and didn't know how to really come in. Everyone felt disconnected and separate. So the job I saw for myself when I came to that school was to bring all of these people together into a village — to bring the wisdom of the village and the drum to facilitate a real shift. It becomes a miracle — a little miracle right there, a very subtle, but very powerful healing.

WHEN I GO INTO THE CORPORATE WORLD, the business world, I say money is good, but if you do well, you do better by doing good. I say to the corporate community that it is okay for the heart to drive the business. Money is a resource. Money is to be used, not just gathered. Everyone in the corporation or in the business is part of

a village and that corporate village is part of the larger village we all live in. We are part of, not separate from, the global community and we are responsible for our place in that community.

Corporate leaders, managers, secretaries, can come into a place of the heart, a place beyond fear, a place of love, a place of sincerity, and a place of clarity. Money is a good thing. Money is a blessing as long as we live here on earth. We cannot take money to any other planetary body or any other dimension or heavenly body. When we die, we leave it all here. We are blessed and gifted by our ancestors who utilized resources with wisdom. It is good to be responsible and to make good decisions about the effect our work has on the whole village because that is what we will leave behind.

In our working environment we can become afraid and that fear can drive us toward the attraction of money for its own sake. This fear can compel us to follow the wrong direction and to make damaging decisions. We may have our eye on short-term profit and not on the best overall interest of the company. I'm thinking, for instance, of situations where a company may rush a product to market even though there have been tests that show it is not safe. Then a terrible accident happens and someone is hurt or killed, the company must pay out a large settlement, and the name of the company is disgraced. The decisions about bringing that product into the market were made because of following fear instead of following the heart. If sales are not high, individuals are afraid they will lose their jobs and management is afraid their bottom line will look bad and boards of directors are afraid stockholders won't approve of their oversight of the company. So the company doesn't have the safe space it needs to develop the right products for the right reasons.

We need our businesses to come unstuck from their fear and to look at their place in the bigger picture. I think the drum is a very powerful tool to help people in corporations and businesses do this. When the drum awakens them to the true self, they will stand in right alignment with spirit and will do the right thing. They will take a chance. They will take a chance to create a better world for all.

When businesses cannot take a chance they become imprisoned within themselves. The only way to be freed is to be real, to be honest, to be truthful and to put to the side the addiction to the money aspects of business. When those running a business can be sincere and authentic in their hearts, then the shift can take place.

The same applies with government organizations. Look around at what is happening in the world. Global organizations like the United Nations are busy talking and not doing. So what the power of the drum can do is to invoke wisdom. The ancient wisdom of the drum can bring governments into alignment and allow them to be awakened, to come to their senses and not be afraid to follow their hearts to make the right decisions. I believe we can heal old wounds and open our hearts to unconditional compassion to build peaceful communities and nations and to avoid wasteful and destructive wars.

The healing begins in each family to end unresolved issues and ignorance that unconsciously gets passed down from one generation to the next. It is up to parents and elders to guide us with wisdom not hatred and pain.

This is really the drum as the voice of the village, it is speaking to all of us about coming together — sharing rather than being separate. All of us sharing together as one global people.

I HEARD A MOVING STORY ABOUT A MAN who had been doing drugs and wasting his life. He turned his life around and started doing good for his family. He became successful in his business and wanted to give back to the world in some way. He had a call from Spirit to go to Sudan to help with some of the problems plaguing the people there. When he got to Sudan he decided to build a safe place to rescue women and children, because he saw how their lives were being destroyed by factions fighting in their country. He never gave up because he felt it was his mission to save these children and women from being killed by this conflict.

We have many problems that we cause ourselves here in the world. This one man started trying to make a difference. Can you imagine the world if we had hundreds of thousands of people like that man, seeing a need and making a difference? What would the world be like — especially the world in Africa today? When I think about this it reminds me again and again that we need to do more. We haven't scratched the surface as human beings. We can write all the books, make all the movies to save the world, but we are only talking. So it is always in my heart that I want to do more in the world. What will awaken the heart, the soul and the body to a realization of peace in the world?

I WAS IN NIGERIA DURING THE BIAFRAN NIGERIAN WAR. I saw terrible things that broke my heart. What happens in our soul that lets us do things like this to each other?

We have to bring Spirit into the center of our lives. Healing and transformation can't take place if we are blocked from the love in our hearts. I feel hurt inside because I know there must be more I can do. I try to use the drum and the gifts that I have to do the best that I can to reach as many as I can. I try to make a difference by going out and doing the work, not just speaking about it.

I yearn for us to come to our senses and stand in a place of love. That's what Life has intended for us. We are not the Author of Life so it is not our right to destroy life. We need to come into right relation to Spirit and bring Spirit into the center of our lives. If we are living out of Spirit we will know what we need to do. Spirit comes into our hearts as a vibration, a sound. It can come as dance or storytelling. It can come as simple generosity like giving another person a glass of water.

THE ROOTS OF A TREE signify the many-faceted aspects of our lineage in relation to the new era of modern civilizations. The roots make up the living foundation that sustains our ecosystems and life. These roots give vitality and sustenance to the human race. The roots also represent different aspects of the divine self and the unexplained mysteries that entwine and bless our coexistence.

This source of power and energy is the sound of the drum, which consists of the elements of earth, fire, water, wind. It is light and air as color and sound. The echo of the drum permeates through soul and body. Healing that needs to happen — be it healing of grief, depression, illness, or physical ailments — can occur through the healing drum and dance.

Imagine yourself in the village where people look you in the eyes, greet you kindly, and ask how you really are. Imagine yourself in this place, this village where people feel sincerely trusting and they care for you and for each other.

The people in the village are sitting around the fire preparing food for the evening. The atmosphere is filled with sounds of music, people talking, chanting, dancing, laughing, eating and drinking.

Imagine the voices of children singing, clapping their hands, playing together, and having fun. Food is being prepared, before everyone eats and drinks from one bowl and one cup. This is a sacred moment of love and bonding, nurturing unity in the spirit of the village.

FOOD IS A CELEBRATION!

The way you are welcomed into a home in the village is with a celebration of food — especially the kola nut tradition that is used to welcome you to the village, to a home, or for a meeting.

Eating the Nigerian way shares similar food traditions with other African societies on the continent and the world. Traditional foods like cassava, yams, plantains and rice that form the foundations of meals might be similar, but our perspective about food is festive and celebratory. Family and community events are celebrated with a variety of delicious foods, native wines, and music. When we gather to eat, bowls of yams or plantains pounded into a paste are brought out along with soups and stews, steamed bean cakes, fish or meat, a vegetable from the garden, and a big pot of tea. We scoop the yam or plantain with our fingers, then this pounded yam paste is dipped into the soup and eaten. Yes, we do have forks and spoons but what is the fun of that? Other delicious treats we are served are moi-moi and suya. Moi-moi is a steamed bean cake. Suya is a brochette with thin slices of grilled cow or goat meat.

EVERYONE WAITS FOR THE HOST AND HOSTESS of the meal to taste the food before it is served to everyone — this custom is similar to the celebration cutting and eating of a piece of wedding cake by the bride and groom before it is served to the guests.

When the host and hostess smile and encourage everyone to serve themselves, the celebration begins! Tea is served.

Many of the typical Igbo foods and recipes are of soups eaten with meat or fish served with either pounded yam, eba (garri which comes from the cassava trees), semovita or jollof rice, and a variety of beans. Real yam is not like the "sweet potatoes" that are called yams in many western countries. True yam is a root, like potatoes, but it is much larger and tastier than potatoes. When a yam is pounded in a mortar, it becomes yam paste. Pounded yam paste is dipped into the soup and eaten. Most of the soups are palm oil based. The most popular foods in the Igboland are:

- EGUSI SOUP : yellowish soup based on melon seeds

- OKRO SOUP : sticky "draw" soup prepared from sliced okro pods

- BITTER SOUP : with bitterleaf but very similar to spinach

- OGBONO SOUP : another 'draw' soup is based on ogbono pods

- ORA AND OGRI SOUP : a vegetable-based soup, mostly eaten in villages

- VEGETABLE SOUP : the exclusive soup for vegetarians, containing a great variety of delicious different vegetables.

Meat or fish are essential components of most soups using meat from cow, chicken, lamb, goat, turkey, dry fish, and stock fish. Stock fish is air dried codfish that is soaked and cooked in soup. On a special occasion it can be prepared with other foods and served during meetings or gatherings.

Okoro Soup

10 pods of Okro (okra)

Meat or fish

4 tomatoes

1 large onion

3 peppers (or non)

1 cup of crayfish

3 spoonfuls of palm oil

1 stock and salt

Add other seasoning
(garlic, cumin and curry)

1. Trim, wash and cut meat or fish into small pieces and boil with half the onion and salt.

2. Crush together the other half of the onion, crayfish peppers, tomatoes. Add to hot palm oil and meat, and let simmer for five minutes

3. Add the okoro, stock, salt to the soup and cook for another ten minutes (slow/ medium heat)

Soups can be served with pounded yam or garri.

Equsi Soup

Cow, chicken, goat or fish

1 cup of dried shrimp or crayfish

2 cups of tomato paste or fresh ground tomatoes

2½ cups of leafy spinach, bitter leaf or other greens

½ spoon of peppers

1½ cup of palm oil

½ cup of sliced onions

1½ cup of ground egusi seed (or melon seeds)

Bullion/ salt to taste

Cut the meat into bite-sized chunks and add 2 cups of water, ½ teaspoon of salt, onions and bullion to the pot.

Then cook for 20 minutes or when meat is almost tender.

Meanwhile, sauté chopped onions, tomatoes and peppers in palm oil for 10 minutes.

Mix the egusi with water to make a paste, add everything together with the shrimp or the crayfish.

When the meat is fried to a brownish color (optional to fry the meat), add the meat as well to the pot.

Let the soup boil for 25 minutes. Lastly, add bitter leaf or other green leaves (chopped very thinly) 10 minutes before the end of cooking duration.

Egusi soup can be eaten with garri, pounded yam or over rice and yam.

Plantain and Yam

Peel the plantain and yam and slice into pieces.
Fry the plantain or Yam in palm oil with some salt.
When it is brownish, let it cool down and eat.

African Stew

    Meat or fish or tofu

    ½ cup of onions and mushroom

    1 cup of fresh tomatoes or paste

    2 cloves of garlic

    ½ teaspoon of salt

    ½ teaspoon of pepper

    1 teaspoon of curry

    1 bouillon

Cut meat or fish into bite sizes and boil until tender

Saute onions, mushrooms, tomatoes, bouillon and garlic with olive oil

Add meat and curry together to the saute sauce to cook for 25 minutes.

You can eat the plantain or yam with the stew sauce.

ASHIKO

Part Three

WORKING WITH THE DRUM

There is a reason our drums start with the wood of a tree.
Trees have always had mythic qualities that represent our
personal and community stories — the metaphors such as
ancestral inheritance and lineage are depicted in family trees, and
the tree of life, or even the tree in the Garden of Eden. And for the
life of the village, trees were crucial and central to every aspect of
life — everything from beds to spoons and bowls, furniture, art,
and course cooking, fires, buildings, commerce and trade, in fact
everything, even our drums.

12

LISTEN

Trees filled our stories and our dreams at night, along with
being the single most important stable central presence in our
eco-system, directly contributing to our health, medicines, herbal
innovations and discoveries, enabling for treatments and cures of
all kinds of diseases and illnesses. For life in the village, trees are
integral to sustaining life itself.

Given the central place trees hold as a symbol of creation
— the beginning and end of life chapters on the earth — you
can understand that the wisdom that emanated from trees was
contained in the very wood of the drums we played. My Great Uncle
Dey, who crafted these drums understood these wisdom teachings.
The trees all speak the same simple truths:

SEED – everything in life begins with a seed.

NOURISHMENT – as a mother nourishes the infant baby, so
   does the Earth nourish the trees.

GROWTH – natural stages of maturity develop in a healthy environment.

WHOLENESS – all of the elements are integrated and contained within the living, growing tree – this includes water, fire, wind, sunlight, starlight, moonlight, all colors and Earth.

EVERYTHING, INCLUDING US, ORIGINATES AS A SEED. Seed is the core of your existence, it is the soul's foundation, the divine spark of energy moving forward. Seeds are the origin of our world, and the values of fairness, kindness, understanding, respect towards all life forms, and compassion are literally seeds. All of these characteristics are really seeds that grow when planted in our lives.

The key to the wisdom of the trees is the knowledge that whatever seeds you select and plant and cultivate, will grow.

The trees teach us that the health of the tree depends on the health of the mother — the earth — and that caring for yourself must include caring for her wellbeing also. In every situation in which we hope to benefit, to prosper, to receive nourishment, or to ignore the Mother who nourishes us is to damage ourselves — and we learn that to care for her is to care for ourselves.

The flow, or growth, of life to increasing stages of capacity and capability is nature's gift to all living beings. Drumming is our expression of "flow" — our celebration of the gift of life to us. When we participate in creating flow by drumming, Spirit grows within us. We become fluid, connected, and the voice of the drum becomes the conduit and awakening environment, or soundscape, for our personal spiritual development and for planetary change. We become healthy, and we create health — called "healing" — around us.

The trees are the voices of nature, and nature's rhythms are the sound of the drum. In African society, a circle space under a sacred tree is a gathering place for people — these places are revered and respected sites for social and religious ceremonies. Here, the village communities gather for drumming, dancing, prayer, worship, healing, meetings — for every purpose.

Humans enjoy refuge under the tree, and the tree contains all of the elements of life — integrated into one presence, rooted in Earth, reaching into the sky, beautiful, offering protection and wisdom. When one dances and drums under the tree, it is as if the heavens have opened a gateway into transcendence.

The healing presence and energetic presence of the tree fosters both personal and community awareness, and it is this natural growth of awareness as well as speaking the language of Spirit with my drum that was the gift of the trees — the gift that my Grandfather and my great Uncle Dey passed to me.

This gift is for you too! Drumming, the voice of the trees speaking in Spirit, has the capacity to re-align the physical, emotional, mental, and physiological states we experience — including our spiritual and supernatural connections. The Divinity of nature, alive in the trees, shifts consciousness, transcending our inhibitions and fears. The result is inner tranquility, along with evolutionary growth and breakthroughs in your life.

And the message of the drum made from the tree of life? "God is good! Creation is good! Love is good! You are good! Life is good!"

Imagine yourself in a blissful state, receiving sound waves of drumming — songs, chanting, celestial voices and instruments bringing waves of harmony into your body. In this moment, you are experiencing the epiphany of life. Here, there are no limitations, no fears, no doubts or false beliefs. Here there are no inhibitions or distractions preventing your discovery of the fulfillment of your dreams and purpose.

THIS IS YOUR INVITATION to find out how to use the drum in a sacred, healing, transcendental, and transformative way.

You are not just beating the drum! With each tap, each touch, each sound of the drum, you create vibrations that transform physiology.

With the drum you are bringing the gift of your unique vibration to the world. You are a gift that you share, by moving into your center with the drum. And when you move into your center, you are the center of all that is. You can understand that each being is the center of all that is — and that there is no contradiction in this.

Each drum beat speaks the simple truth that we are whole, that we are One. The drum is an agent of transformation, satisfying our deep yearning to recognize the sacred holy presence within us, at our center.

So this is an invitation for you to come on a journey with the drum, to bring the drum within the journey of your life. I invite you to allow yourself this opportunity to discover your own inherent abilities. They are already present and it is just a matter of being motivated to awaken and supported to awaken — to find out for yourself.

13
LISTEN

The music in Africa is not restricted to drums only. There are vast selections of sound instruments that are used for a variety of functions, celebrations, performances, events, and ceremonies. Some rare ancient instruments are used for certain ceremonies such as coronation and festivity. My point is that whatever instruments played during certain functions, those instruments are respected and revered. When you hold an instrument or sit behind a drum you are totally present in that moment and your entire life is held in the song. You are sharing your whole life and everything you are with another person unconditionally and without reservations. The expression of your sound becomes your gift from God to the world. You are in the moment, playing your life through the creation of the most sacred powerful sound ever imagined! This sound is a call to awakening to dwell in and to be consumed by its life-giving force.

CREATE YOUR CONNECTION WITH THE DRUM.

First, sit quietly with your drum. Acknowledge that you are in the presence of the sacred and that you are in a sacred realm. Breathe slowly, noticing the in breath and the out breath. Come fully present.

Second, make a fist with your hand, but do not touch the drum yet. Beating the drum with your fist will hurt you, as well as the drum. The tightly closed fist contains our anger, our violence, our misunderstandings, our hurt, and our despair. We think that it protects us, but we are stressed, uncomfortable, and unable to care for ourselves or others with our tightly held closed fists.

Open your hand, and release this anger — it is an act of forgiveness. Whatever the story, whatever has happened, forgive. Nothing that has happened can justify keeping your fist closed — you are the one continuing the anger and hurt. As you forgive, your hand opens. As you come full circle to unconditional forgiveness, your heart opens.

Third, breathe and allow spirit to come home to the body. Breathe and feel the connection happen. With an open heart, love awakens.

Now, touch the drum, letting the wisdom of the drum vibrate through every cell of your body. This is how drumming is a spiritual practice — the drum becomes the opening to the awakening of the psyche, the opening of the heart, and the connection to the field of infinite potential in your life.

Every one of us has gifts and is gifted, but sometimes we don't open our gifts. The drum now opens the gifts that we didn't even know we had. When I am teaching, and I invite people to dance to the drum, I see people go around and around like little soldiers, then, suddenly they start getting loose, and pretty soon these people, they are alive! You can see that the gift of their life has become present.

Play! Live! Celebrate! Be Alive! Pick up the drum and play it as your celebration of life! Obstructions become transparent, dissolve and fade away. Our joyful awareness of the presence of the sacred awakens.

I AM GOING TO PLAY SOME OF THE DIFFERENT DRUMS and the different drumming patterns so you will come to understand the language of the drum, the message that the drum is speaking. Go to **shamanzone.com** for audio clips of the drumming.

14
LISTEN

When a person in the village has died you can drum out the message that someone important has died. If I were going to send that message from my village I would also sing a song that goes with it.

This traditional drum originated in West Africa especially from the Yoruba land of Nigeria. It has a large hourglass shape with strings roped across on the side of the drum skin. It is played with a drumstick. These drums are used for entertaining guests at weddings and other ceremonies and occassions. It has goatskin heads and a hardwood shell. It also has a shoulder strap and curved stick.

The talking drum is a drum where the pitch can be varied. Like many drums, the talking drum has been used for communication. When the drum is squeezed under the arm and played, one can produce the intonations of human speech or language.

To me, drumming is talking. Can you hear it? I am saying something to you — now I am saying something different.

Can you feel the different sounds in the cells of your body?

15
LISTEN

You can hear the conversation I am playing with my hands. You can talk with any drum and call and respond with any drum. The talking drum specifically communicates a conversation from one person to the other. Actually you can say, "How are you?" with the drum. "I am fine." "I am going to Safeway." Must be the shopping list!

I AM GOING TO TEACH YOU FUNDAMENTAL TECHNIQUES FOR DRUMMING.

The **bass**.

The **open**.

The **slap** sound.

You have the **mute**, which muffles the sound.

Then you have **rolls**, meaning you can roll all the techniques independently.

The **silence** or the space is a very important technique.

So those are the fundamentals.

16

LISTEN

FIRST YOU ESTABLISH THE BASS, THE HEARTBEAT. The **heartbeat** gives you the foundation for everything else you intend to play.

My teaching concepts are organic and simple. You can think of creating a song as a metaphor for your life story.

The bass establishes who you are, your character, your person. The opening sound will give you the opportunity to be flexible, clear, and focused so you can help and support yourself and others. So when you have this combination — the bass and the open together, you have established a good relationship. This connection you create in the rhythms encourages you to have healthier relationships in life.

THE MONORHYTHM AND THE POLYRHYTHMS.

The **monorhythm** is one rhythm played at a time.

The **polyrhythm** is two rhythms played simultaneously together.

Think of it as interacting as good citizens of our community and the world. We are having a conversation on issues that we care about. We are telling our own stories. Everyone in the universe has a story to tell. Even a child in the womb has his or her own story, and the story must be heard. So one of the most important aspects of rhythm and drumming is communication. It teaches how to listen and respond patiently with love, openness, and kindness. An important aspect of this theme is giving and receiving with an open heart — how to really communicate what you mean to say.

17
LISTEN

When you come to play the drum, don't be angry, but instead be pleasant. You can prepare yourself spiritually through meditation. You come with gratitude, with respect, deep love, nobility, and integrity. When you play and how you play the drum gives you the freedom to fully live. If you are patient with the drum, it communicates a whole different sound to the person listening or dancing. I am hoping that those listening to this will be blessed with understanding of the wisdom of the drum and will then pass this message on to the world.

THE CENTER OF OUR LIFE IS THE HEARTBEAT. Our heartbeat reminds us that we are ourselves a drum beating out the rhythms of our personal lives, connecting our one life to the One life of all of us together.

We just let the drums speak.

ONYE AND FAMILY OF DRUMS

SOMEONE IN THE VILLAGE IS SICK and this same person is having a problem with his finances, or with a friend, or in his work. He is wanting his body to heal, and he is also seeking a solution to these conflicts in his life. In the village, instead of taking this man to the hospital, we place him in the center of the square where people gather round him with different types of drums beating out different rhythms. All the drums are playing continuously at the same time.

Here's an example of the Unity Dance. You dance the Unity Dance because you have the story of the pum, pump pum, pum, dun, dun, dun, dun dun and so on. So, the Unity Dance rhythm draws more from a traditional rhythm.

This traditional way of healing calls the spirit of the drum to wake up the cells in the body to the inspiration of the Holy Spirit, what we call the healing breath of God. This will go on for a day or two or three — maybe even a week or two weeks — nonstop. The body is entraining to the natural vibration of the drum. Remember that in the beginning of this ritual the songs and the dancing and the rhythms playing at the same time help set the intention to heal. Imagine what is happening to the entire physical body system — the heart, liver, pancreas, lungs, kidney, gallbladder, cranium and sacrum. It is a process of sanctification through the sound waves and sound healing of the drum.

No one can really determine how the cure comes, but it does come. It is still a mystery. There is a time in the rhythm and dance and songs where the one being healed transcends into an unchartered consciousness where this one merges with the angels into the light of Divinity. That's where miracles happen. The sound awakens the one being healed into alignment with the Divine.

If you are depressed, grieving, or saddened about things you can't understand or can't resolve, the sound of the drum can open you up and allow you to release the energy knots or blocks stored in your body. These knots may represent things you have not forgiven about yourself, or about others, or any sort of unfinished business. It might even represent the past imprint of soul memories that you may have carried in your body since you were born or even before

18

LISTEN

you were born. The time to let these blocks go is during the power of the drum so you can say yes to life. You can say, "Yes, I am ready to move forward into my authentic story, my authentic alignment with the Divine." And now you can say this clearly and profoundly with your body and your life, without words. The conversation is with the sound, with songs and with clear vision and profound intention that you will be restored to balance and wholeness and wellness.

19
LISTEN

When certain specific rhythms are targeted to affect certain locations in the body, the drum can purify toxic or negative influences. When people drum, laugh and cry, sing and dance together, they heal and feel joyful. Optimism is renewed. Together, we celebrate Life!

SOMETIMES WHEN I AM HEALING WITH THE DRUM a green
light or aura can be seen around my hands and body. This light is
the light of the universe. It is the starlight of sounds that permeate
into my energy field and are then transmitted back to my healing
work in the world. When you are in alignment with the heartbeat of
the sacred universe the drum sounds can be seen as colors as well
as heard as sound. They can translate into love and celebration.

Here is the sound of the light of the universe. Can you hear the
green light? Listen for the green . . . it goes "krrrr . . ."

When I play the drum or another instrument, my body and my
soul dwell in the sacred heart of the Divine. Music is a place of
worship and an act of worship singing praise to the Lord. It is an
opportunity to surrender completely without reservations and fear.
The sound rhythms that come out of me are many combinations
of the seven elements — earth, fire, water, mineral, ether, light
and air. The sounds include spectrums of colors as well. The
creative, spontaneous and innovative expressions of sound inspire
a moment of ecstatic music. That moment is like drinking fresh
spring water and smelling fragrant red roses. It is an infinite flow of
the vibrant life force. I am in an awakened state, and my entire body
therefore surrenders unconditionally. When my hands are moving

very, very fast, I feel at peace and relaxed. The multi-faceted sound is being transmitted into my soul. It makes me feel energized, alive and well, but never tired.

As my energy increases with the drumming I can feel my body waking up to a heightened awareness of everything happening in the present moment— it is an expanded or awakened consciousness. It is all a mystery to me. I just go with the flow without analyzing.

PREPARING TO DRUM AND TO DANCE is a whole different process from actually drumming and dan practice and a journey to self-discovery ar realization. You go up to the mountain to affirm your intent and to sanctify yourself through fasting and prayers. There are no excuses— no procrastination. When you drum and dance the blessings that come you truly reach out through you to others. things come full circle and the blessings t come to others in this way reach through back to bless you as well.

DJEMBE

About ten years ago when I was perfor drum concert, as I started up to the stage got very warm and then hot. When I open concert with an invocation on my Djembe my hands were so hot and I was playing s that my Djembe caught on fire. The audie was startled, but excited. During my visio I am sometimes shown different music compositions and dance movements. The dances and the rhythms are revealed to m bright colors and light. And the dances that are revealed are related to the rhythms and the rhythms determine the dance. It is complex and yet very simple.

20

LISTEN

PEOPLE WITH MENTAL ILLNESS OR DEPRESSION can benefit from prayers and positive words. In some countries, mental health institutions use an alternative to medication to help patients with disturbances in the mind and body. For example, Turkey uses a special flute called a Ney.

When a patient hears that sound, the patient's body shifts as the flute sound resonates through his entire system.

The body is such a powerful, mysterious gift given to us by the Creator and by the Universe, and its health is our responsibility. Too often we abuse the body with unhealthy substances and an unhealthy lifestyle. When we abuse our body we disrespect the Creator and the Universe. We disrespect the Creator constantly, and at the same time we call on the Creator to mend our lives and hear our prayers. When we enter the sound of the drum, we align ourselves again with the Divine so we can be whole in this body and give praise and thanks.

In the beginning, God manifested his glory with the "Word" to create the universe. The Word was a vibration, a sound — the first pulse of the drum of manifestation. The Word of God is the universal sound that gives life to all living creatures to coexist. Creation is a wave of consciousness and intention that may be considered an energetic vibration. It creates and affects all vital elements — earth, water, fire, air — as well as the cycle of the seasons. It effects everything that grows, including the transitions from one phase of our lives to another.

This vibration and sound touches everyone on the earth — we breathe, smell, taste, eat, drink, embrace, nourish, love, and are loved from the beloved sacred sound of the drum according to the source of life.

THIS IS HERE FOR YOU. You can come alive when you drum under the celestial heavens. Through vibration, communication is established among all things. The gateway opens to far distant worlds, to expanded senses — to love and revelation.

With my drum, I pray for you:

We are the children of the universe, no less than the stars, the moon, and sun. We are the mysteries, and we are the divinity of nature. We are privileged to be here. Rest in the natural great peace of God. Share kindness, and love warmly. Celebrate your life!

AFRICAN DRUMS

I n West Africa, the drum is the most important instrument for Nigerians, and especially the indigenous Igbo people. The natural instrument is generally used during celebrations, festivities, rites of passage, funerals, rituals and ceremonies, war, village town meetings, important announcements, and an array of other pertinent events. Since the origin of drums, many, many types of drums have been be crafted and perfected over the years.

UDO (ALSO KNOW AS KIM KIM)

The traditional Igbo Udo drum is a clay or metal pot drum with attached grass-woven ring base. Udo drums come from the eastern states of of Nigeria and are played by complimentary instruments such as an Ekwe (log drum), Bells, and Shaker.

The Udo drum is a pot drum made of clay and traditionally played with either the hand or a foam paddle. The Udo drums can serve as bass drum with melodic tone or as in the bass guitar. To achieve a low and deep sound, a minimal amount of water is added. Also, to maintain a higher sound, a modest amount of water is added to the pot as well. Now, to play this instrument, musicians will place it between the legs and grip the neck with the left hand. In order to produce sound, the player will cup her hand and strike the opening very quickly.

To produce sound with an Udo with two holes (top and side) place your palm on the top hole, allowing for control over the drum's pitch as the other hand strikes the side holes and creates an incredible tone. Usually, this instrument is played by women and for female gatherings. Also, it is used for traditional rites of passage, initiations, weddings, and community club meetings and special events.

21
LISTEN

SLIT DRUM (EKWE)

This slit drum is called Ekwe and is also very popular in the Igbo culture. This drum is constructed from a hollowed pear tree trunk. Once the trunk has been cleaned, two horizontal slits are carved into the base as well as a narrow slit connecting the two. The Ekwe comes in a variety of sizes and designs and each size is determined by its functions and purpose.

The drum is played by a solid wood stick that can produce distictive sound. Usually it is used to warn the community of danger, music, and important announcements such as emergencies. The Ekwe is used as a wood type of talking drum to communicate long distance messages to villages far and beyond. The only difference is that it does not have "call waiting" or "redial" features.

22
LISTEN

GONGS CALLED OGENE AND OLU (IGBO BELLS)

These instruments are an integral part of the Igbo musical heritage and culture. They are one of the most prominent and populous musical instruments for both the Olu and Ogene. The Olu is a is large gong and about four feet long. The Ogene is a smaller eight inch long gong. Its main function is mostly for complimenting drums and other percussion instructions. The Olu gong especially has a very unique and distinctive sound this is also used to warn village people of any state of emergency. I did remember it when I was a child. In fact, I have used it to warn people of dangers and announcements in the village.

23
LISTEN

AFRICAN GOURD CALABASH

24

LISTEN

This particular style of calabash or gourd has a variety of uses and functions in traditions and cultures around the world. Although its origin is West Africa, today it is found in the Americas and the Caribbean. It is a fruit of varied shape and size, and it commonly grows on vines, not unlike the squash. There is also varieties of the fruits that grow in bushes and trees. In African cultures and societies, the calabash has historically and traditionally been used used as a container and for fetching water, grains, and other food items. It is mostly used as a utensil in many parts of the world. "When I was growing up, my brothers, sister, and I ate and drank from the calabash. Usually, the taste of the calabash blended with the food develops a whole different taste. I can still remember the taste to this day . . . waah, it is very refreshing. The memory of these sensations brought me back to my village — instant life experiences! It's awesome! Throughout Africa, Asia, the Pacific Islands, the Caribbean and the Americas, gourds are used as resonators/ vibrations for musical instruments.

To create a water calabash for musical instruments is very simple. Pour some amount of water into an empty big calabash and cover it with another smaller calabash. The top calabash floats on the water and at this time you can use your fist to pound on the calabash. However, it can be played without water, turn the empty calabash face down. Play on the top of the calabash with your fists. The electromagnetic sound of the calabash is very mesmerizing and deep resonating effects captivate your entire body and soul with euphoric bliss.

SHAKER / SHEKERE (IGBO AND YORUBA, NIGERIA)

Shakers / Shekere are found throughout the continent of Africa and called different names but it is predominantly known from the Igbo and Yoruba land in the eastern and western Nigerian regions. The shekere is made from various sized gourds that grow on the ground. The shape of the gourd determines the sound of the instrument. A shekere is made by drying the gourd for several months and removing the pulp and seeds. After it is scrubbed, a colorful netting of bead work is covered to the outside to produce a "shaker-like sound." It is a great instrument to accompany a wide range of percussion instruments.

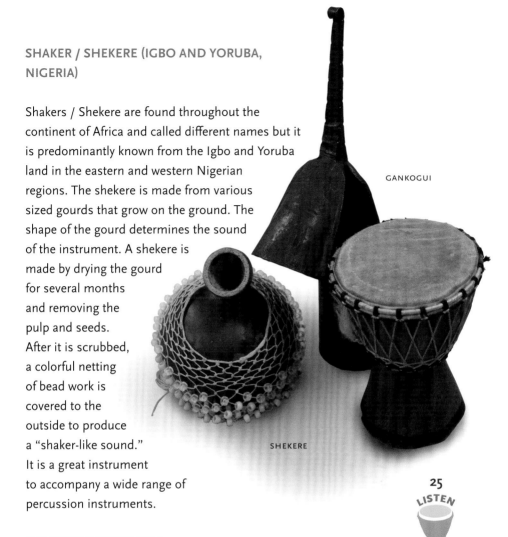

GANKOGUI

SHEKERE

25
LISTEN

GANKOGUI / IRON BELL

The Gankogui is a double bell played with a wooden stick. It is made of forged iron and consists of a low-pitched bell (referred to as the parent bell) and a high pitched bell (referred to as the child bell), which are permanently bound together. The Gankogui is the foundation and core of the Ewe music. The Gahkogui player must play steadily and consistently throughout the duration of the drumming. The player is considered trustworthy person because he is responsible for the entire drumming music.

DJEMBE DRUM

The migration of the Djembe drum from Guinea into the Gambia, Senegal, and Mali has made this drum and its rhythms widely known in West Africa. It is played at the spiritual, healing, and social ceremonies of many tribes. The djembe rhythm and dance tradition is being taught throughout Europe and the United states today as a performing art.

The djembe body is carved and hollowed out by hand from a bush mango tree from the West African forest. The mango tree is a very lightweight wood that makes these drums easy to transport. A goat skin obtained from ceremonial practices or from a goat killed for its meat is strung by hand onto the wooden shell and "pulled." The shape of the shell creates a deep resonance of lower tones, while its popular high pitched tones can be enhanced by tightening the skin with heat or by "pulling" the ropes. Multiple tones can be played. For a long time now many, many African countries are making Djembe drums and other instruments.

26

LISTEN

ASHIKO DRUM (YORUBA, NIGERIA)

27

LISTEN

The Ashiko drum was originally played by the Yoruba people of Nigeria and was carved out of a solid log wood. It is a drum shaped like a cone and meant to be played with your hands. Ashiko is played in Nigeria and throughout sub-Saharan Africa and eastern Cuba. It is designed and carved in a variety of sizes and shapes. In Cuba it is known as "Boku" and it is played during carnivals and street parades.

NGOMA DRUMS

Ngoma in Swahili means "drum."
It is a traditional musical instrument
from East Africa. It has an intriguing
history and was the source of
communication between the King and
his people. It is made from a hollowed
wooden shape with a cow skin placed
on the top and bottom of the drum and
tightened to secure great sound effects. There
are other styles of Ngoma drums with skin over
the drum head and tightly wound with rope to
create deeper and high pitched sound.

    The Ngoma is used for communications, dances, and official
ceremonies as well as special events. The Ngoma is, for example,
used to announce the start of a wedding ceremony.

28
LISTEN

THE NGOMA STORY OF THE NGOMA

In the previous eras before Tanzania got its independence there
were about eight kingdoms in the Buhaya region. Traditionally,
each king would receive a spear and a Ngoma drum to symbolize
authority. The king would use this Ngoma to communicate with
the community. However, the different sounds of the drum can
communicate a variety of meanings and functions such as war,
poor weather conditions, emergencies, new farming and hunting
seasons, attacks from neighboring kingdoms, or the announcement
of birth and deaths. This Ngoma represents the king's power and
is protected by a special guard. During the rein of a King, and if the
Ngoma drum is stolen by another Kingdom, the king would lose
power and would be forced to join another Kingdom. In Uganda,
the people of Baganda have a special relationship to Ngoma drum.
People have traditionally thought that the Ngoma drum originated
from the Baganda tribe. They have popularized the Ngoma drum
tradition in western and European societies.

MBIRA (THUMB PIANO)

The thumb piano of the Shona tribe in Zimbabwe. It is played by locking metal strips on a wooden slab, often clamped inside a gourd resonator. Used for social, spiritual, ceremonial, and festive occasions.

29
LISTEN

BREKETA/ GONGON – (BASS SNARE DRUM)

30
LISTEN

Great bass snare from Ghana, similar to Nigerian Djun Djun barrel bass drum. They are lightweight and made from a single piece of hardwood carved thin and a double headed bass drum with goat skin on both sides. Snare string is stretched across the skin. It is traditionally played in the same position as a talking drum, in the armpit, and comes with a traditional curve stick. Typically the drum is covered with colorful African cloth.

BOBA DRUM

Boba was invented by the Ewe tribe of Ghana in the 1950s to assist in the newly composed song called Gahu. It is a wide drum and is the lowest and deepest sounding drum of the Ewe drums from Ghana.

31
LISTEN

KIDI SUPPORT DRUM

The Kidi is a mid-size drum played with two wooden sticks. It functions mostly as a supporting drum and uses the same technique as the Sogo drum. The Kidi does what is described by the Ewe as "talking" or "conversing" with the lead drum. It is similar in shape to the Sogo but smaller, and a little higher in pitch.

32
LISTEN

YORUBA OMELE AKO BATA

Omele AKO Bata Drum is one of the Bata Drum family (male backing drums). Three small bata with three basic language tones. These three drums are tied together and are kplayed by one drummer using two flat animal leather beaters. It creates a variety of low, medium and high pitched sound enhancing the quality of the music.

33
LISTEN

SAKARA

The Sakara drum is one of the major family of Youba drums of Nigeria.
It is commonly known as a shallow drum with a circular body made with baked clay. The Yoruba have traditionally used Sakara for a variety of reasons and functions. Like any drum, a king could use it to summon people to court, or to a wedding ceremony. They were also used to announce visitors to the King or for official event for broadcasting messages, and for speaking prayers. The Sakara is also created and played by the Hausa people from the Northern Regions.

34
LISTEN

35
LISTEN

TALKING DRUMS
NIGERIAN (YORUBA)
VARIETY PITCH

An hourglass-shaped, variable-pitch drum from the Yoruba states of Nigeria. These drums are used for entertaining guests at weddings and other ceremonies and occassions. It has goatskin heads, a hardwood shell, and a shoulder strap with a curved stick.

The talking drum is drum where the pitch can be varied. Like many drums, the talking drum has been used for communicating. When the drum is squeezed under the arm and played, one can produce the intonations of human speech or language. This traditional drum originated in West Africa, especially from the Yoruba land of Nigeria.

36　TAMA (WOLOF NAME FOR TALKING DRUM) (SENEGALESE)

LISTEN

This Tama talking drum has a variable pitch. Its Dimba wood shell is carved in an hourglass shape. A tightly wound cotton cord is used for changing pitch. This is done by squeezing the drum under one of the player's arms while tapping one of its heads with the curved stick in the opposite hand. The heads are usually lizard skin. It is played with a curved stick.

NOTE : *If played live, all talking drums sound best amplified through a microphone. It has a wide, profound, deep, and expressive tonal range.*

IGBO WORDS AND PHRASES

ABU (AYBOO) : Dance

CHINEKE (CHIN NEE KEE) : The supreme God

EGUSI SEEDS (EGOO SEE) : Melon seeds used in African dishes

EGWU (EGOO) : Dancing and singing to drumming

EMELA (EE MAY LA) : "Thank you."

ERI GBOLA (EERY BOLAY) : One of the traditional Igbo greetings. "How is your dancing?"

ORI MA (OREE MA) : Response to the greeting "I feel good/ healthy." "I am well."

NAIRA (NIE RA) : The main unit of currency in Nigeria

KOBO : 100 Kobo are in one Naira

CULTURE OF NIGERIA

INTRODUCTION

Because of its great diversity of people and culture, Nigeria has distinguished herself over the centuries in the field of arts. Nigerian versatility in art is so great that it is generally felt that all African nations should view Nigeria as the principal trustee of the most durable fruits of black artistic genius. It is not precisely known when the first works of Nigerian art reached the outside world, but in 1897, following a British punitive expedition to Bcnin, over 2,000 Benin bronzes and ivories were shipped to England and later dispersed all over Europe and America. The oldest sculptures found in Nigeria were from the Southern Zaria and Benue areas of central Nigeria. They consist of terracotta figures and figurines made by a people who achieved a high degree of cultural sophistication. These sculptures, together with other cultural elements, have been attributed to the Nok Culture. Evidence shows the Nok people had knowledge of iron smelting and adorned themselves with tin and stone beads, earrings, noserings and bracelets. The Nok Culture is dated between 500 BC and 200 AD.

AMBER NECKLACE

THE NEXT KNOWN PHASE OF NIGERIAN CULTURAL EVOLUTION was Igbo Ukwu bronze casting. Found in the small village of Igbo-Ukwu, near Awka, the casts date from the 9th century AD. They first came to light in 1938 and consist of staff heads, crowns, breastplates, pendants, ornaments, anklets, wristlets, and chains. About the same time the Igbo-Ukwu people were casting bronze, the ancient Ife people were also producing works in bronze, copper, and terracotta. In the first quarter of this century, Iife works caused a great stir among world art critics and historians who were unaccustomed to such naturalism in African art. The best known Nigerian artworks are the Benin Antiquities. Legend recounts how the Benin people learned the art of bronze casting from Ile-Ife around 1400 AD. Oba Ogunta, the sixth King of Benin, is credited with having encouraged this art in Benin. Nigeria's cultural heritage is woven from threads of history and diversity, legend and conquest. Tourists visiting the country will gain insights in to a glorious past as well as a promising future, set amid the natural beauty of this diverse country. From rain forests in the south, broad savanna woodlands in the center, to a semi-desert region in the north, Nigeria offers a remarkable range of physical beauty in her land as well as the generous hospitality of her people, ready to be enjoyed by the tourist fortunate enough to choose this land of ancient empires as their travel destination. Nigeria is a vast country with a population of about 170,124,000 people covering about 923,768 SQ KM of landmass, located wholly within the tropics. The country aptly described as the "Giant of Africa" is richly endowed with ecological and cultural resources, which are of universal recognition. The richness and diversity of the Nigerian culture is a manifestation of the socio-cultural differences of the over 250 ethnic groups that have inhabited the land for ages.

KANO DYE PITS

The Kano indigo-vegetable dye pits are one of the most fascinating aspects of this old city. Various designs are folded into the material before dyeing, and the fabric is often beaten to achieve the shiny, iridescent appearance. The techniques employed to obtain this look are unmatched around the world. And although the methods they use are ancient, these lush works of art on fabric always remain extremely popular and continue to be in great demand.

LEATHER WORK

Nigeria is a veritable treasure trove of beautiful handmade crafts. Drawing from ancient traditions, Nigerian artisans create marvelous wood carvings, metal castings, exotic jewelry, traditional clothing, intricately decorated calabashes, and finely-crafted leatherwork. Visitors are amazed at the quality and value of these unique creations, each made with a perfectionist's skill and attention to detail.

HISTORICAL AND CULTURAL FACTS

Nigeria is one of the wealthiest, most influential, and popular countries in black Africa. Its variations of land and hot, moist climate range from thick mangrove swamps to beautiful beaches and dense rainforests. The river Niger, which flows to the sea through a great delta in Nigeria, links the savanna and forest. For centuries, it was the route through which the population and cultures interrelated.

Nigeria has a remarkable cultural and historical richness. Archaeologists and historians have found ancient statues and artifacts that reveal a rich and complex artistic and cultural heritage. There are three major ethnic groups in Nigeria that speak more than 250 different dialects and languages. Roughly 2/3 of them speak Hausa, Yoruba and Igbo, but the official language is English, which is based on African grammar and is widely used in the cities, towns, and villages.

Agricultural products such as cotton, cocoa, rubber, yams, cassava, corghum, palm kernels, millet, corn, kola, rice, and livestock are cultivated on the village farms. Igboland is in the southeast portion of Nigeria, which has been inhabited since the dawn of recorded history. The Igbo are known for their ambition to improve themselves. They are a people with a heritage of respect for life, family roots, and education. They have a strong sense of community and responsibility. Their cultural and spiritual life is very important to them. They believe that health, longevity, and prosperity are gifts given in return for their prayers, sacrifices and blessings. Children are considered to be the greatest blessing of all. Everyone, no matter how young or old, contributes something to the nourishment and wellbeing of the family and community.

TRADITIONAL AFRICAN CULTURE

The historical richness of an African culture gives a sense of family and community. In the village, we live with an extended family of grandparents, parents, children, brothers, sisters, cousins, aunts, and uncles. Family structure is one of the many important systems among Africans. Most of the marriages are arranged by the parents of the bride and groom to be. They are arranged for the health, happiness and unity of both families.

The marriage ceremony signifies the beginning of one of the principal rituals in Africa, which marks the continuation of life. While both men and women are important in the upbringing and care of the children, the women play a central role in the family, raising the children, trading goods, and handling household and business matters.

Today, both African men and women are advancing themselves through higher education and by learning vocational and professional skills. Everyday in the village, families gather to talk about the events of the day. Even the youngest child gets a chance to tell his/her story. All elders are honored and cared for. They teach and pass on wisdom to the following generations through storytelling and by sharing proverbs, poetry, music, and art. Many of the stories remind children and adults of the moral lessons of life.

Music, drums, dances, songs, folklore, and drama have always been a way of life for Africans. Drum and dance are powerful ways to communicate thoughts, express feelings and emotions with deep sense of building unity and communities. Drums are used to create music and to announce significant gatherings, news, and events in many villages. They are also used at birth, where they accompany naming and rites of passage ceremonies where all the extended families and relatives welcome the child with full honor, a blessings and celebration.

RITES OF PASSAGE

In ancient tribal societies, native African children before and near the time of puberty underwent various individual and communal passages into adulthood. These rites were performed immediately following birth and also separately for boys and girls between 9–17 years old. Today, our modern society is lacking in rites of passage for individuals of all ages as they experience stages of development. We have few ceremonies, such as graduations and marriage, that prepare our soul profoundly or mark significant transitions in life. However, rites of passage from indigenous cultures offer powerful ways for children, teenagers, and even adults to honor their initiations and transitions with a sense of meaning, purpose, and destiny. These rites instill a sense of individuality and community while developing and nurturing a healthy psyche.

IGBO PEOPLE

Igbo people find their home in a rich and fertile crescent created by the lower Niger River within Nigeria. Their population has presently grown to around thirty million people. Within all of Africa, the Igbo homelands are probably one of the most densely populated regions. It is believed by many that this area and its people were one of the driving forces in the early development of the Iron Age which has helped mold the world as we know it. Their culture has brought much to enrich the world.

When looking at the history of Igbo political life, one may get a sense of its complexity. Compared to many other areas of Africa, their government seems disjointed to some. At the bottom levels of their government there is a common and distinct policy concerning representation. Within the Igbo community, if a group does not have a representative to share their views, they are not heard. It is a kind of democracy that has survived British influences from various contacts. Representation at the community level is maintained equally as each tries to contribute resources that would help further the community in its tasks. In turn, all rules and regulations made within each village and community traditionally are only applied to that village. The laws stay within the walls in which they were created.

Today the majority of Igbo are of the Christian belief. They are probably the largest group of Christians within the whole continent of Africa. Before Christianity was introduced, their belief system revolved around one particular god, named "Chukwu." The Igbo's beliefs were once very tribal in nature. Although many of the smaller deities would compete among themselves, they would always stay within their realm of activity. With Chukwu being seen as an all-powerful and omnipresent God, representations, symbols, and sanctuaries could be found almost anywhere. Homes, compounds, buildings and even village parks and squares would display these depictions of Chukwu. Due to the diversity of the Igbo language, the sanctuaries are referred to by many different names. CHI was seen individually and was personalized by its followers. The people believed strongly in one's ability to improve status in the present world or afterlife through change. Many point out that these traits may have made a smoother transition to the current Christian community.

The Igbo have a very unique and distinctive language. It is said often to be one of the hardest to learn. The difficulty of the language often stems from the fact that it is not spoken anywhere else in the world. It is a rich language with many variations. With heavy cultural roots directed at change for the better, the Igbo seem to be just as diverse as the changing language they speak. Igbo home life is also very structured. Typically the husband is the head of the household. He also accepts his responsibilities to his community. It is of equal importance to tend to both the family and the village. Igbo people usually have very extended families; it is a part of them as a people. In recent years, there has even been a drive for family members who have moved away to return to their origin of birth, along with their new offspring. The Igbo people have stood out in their own way throughout their history. Within Nigeria, they have pooled together with enthusiasm and accomplishment as a people who take pride in themselves and their history. With a distinct language and culture, they will continue to grow as a people.

References:

Uchendu Victor C. THE IGBO OF SOUTHEAST NIGERIA. New York: Holt, Rinehard and Winston, Inc, 1965.

Okere, L.C. The Anthropology of Food in rural Igboland, Nigeria. London: University Press of America, Inc. 1983

Nigeria and the Igbo Culture (05/08/2000) http: //www.geocities. com/Athens/Acropolis/ 3629/-04/29/00 Written by: Matt VanderSluis

Acknowledgements

I want to offer a special thank you to Frank Hayhurst, my dear friend, mentor and guide who ceaselessly inspired and motivated me to tell my story. I also thank Paulette Millichap whose belief in this book was essential to its development.

I want to thank John Records who has so enthusiastically inspired and supported my desire to write this book.

I especially want to thank Robert Marcus who provided most of the photographs for this book, as well as his friendship and tireless support.

My deepest gratitude goes out to my dear friend, Larry Berkeley, for his generosity, especially during our years at the College of the Holy Cross, and for his contagious humor, laughter and encouragement. I also thank David and Eileen Perini for their sponsorship, love, compassion, and education.

Thank you to the Spirit of The Drum and the Heart and Soul of The Almighty.

Go to **www.villagerhythms.com** to contact Onye Onyemaechi for music, drum programs, educational programs, and consulting for business and organizations.

Go to **www.insightsforhealing.com** to contact Onye for personal development, spiritual consulting and healing, and for booking events and gatherings around the world.

Go to **www.shamanzone.com/onye** for audio and video clips from this book, and contact francis@shamanzone.com for additional information.

LISTEN

*May the Peace and the Light of the Universe rest upon your
heart and soul as you read* The Drum, Voice of the Village.

*As you hear the sound of the drum, it will eliminate all of your
concerns or worries day to day — and it will empower you and
strengthen you, and will invigorate your consciousness in ways you
have never experienced before.*

*I wish you the holiness and the desire to shine in the world —
and to become who you are, and feel and live a worthwhile life with
joy and peace.*

*Peace I give to you, and love remains in your heart and soul —
this I wish for you.*

Peace, Shalom, Salam, Aho, Amen

Onye Onyemaechi School Presentations

It is with great pleasure that I recommend Onye Onyemaechi's African Village Celebration for your school . . . With his drums and trunk full of West African culture he brought us back to a feeling of community . . . Wisdom, love, respect, relaxation and celebration were all qualities experienced by our school during this exceptional program.

> • NANCY C. MANNION, The Discovery Center School, San Francisco

Onye teaches about African culture through the use of dance, music and costumes. He has a magical way of getting an entire high school actively participating with him during the performance. Onye's philosophy emphasizes sound values, respect for others, and the "celebration of life." Onye's assembly positively affected more students and faculty than any other performer we have had here.

> • J. ROSS THAYER, Director of Student Activities, R. L. Stevenson School, Pebble Beach, California

Onye Onyemaechi is a remarkable talent. The spirit and vitality in his music bask the listener in a joyful glow.

> • BETH MAURENCE, KBAC FM

Onye Onyemaechi and his Village Rhythms performances are inspiring, energetic and just plain fun! He is able to engage the entire audience with his music and stories. The show is both interactive and educational. Onye brings his warm smile, great talent, positive energy and truly wonderful percussion music to all of his shows.

> • JENNIFER WEEKS, Librarian, Campbell Library.

Onye Onyemaechi Corporate Presentations

Onye Onyemaechi has created a unique and dynamic workshop that can have a dramatic and exciting effect on today's corporate organizations. His enthusiasm, wisdom, and sense of humor can stimulate a work group so effectively that managers may be astonished by the change in their staff. Productivity, interpersonal skill, and group effectiveness can all see a measurable gain.

> • BILL GIOVINO, President, CPU Technologies of Boston

Onye not only gives us the thrilling African drumming/ dancing experience, he weaves traditional village wisdom into modern group interaction and management problem solving.

> • ROBERT MARCUS, marketing director, Environmental Pollution Abatement Co., Inc., Santa Rosa

Onye is great, and drumming is a wonderful way to integrate people. I had the pleasure of working with Onye Onyemaechi professionally. I would highly recommend Onye and drumming to corporate clients as a team building exercise, particularly when you want to pull people from different departments/areas/expertise together to build a cohesive team!

> • LAUREL COOTE, corporate event and meeting manager, Los Angeles, California.

To contact Onye Onyemaechi go to **www.villagerhythms.com**